STAR WARS

BE MORE LANDO

Written by Christian Blauvelt

Contents

The stylish path to the top

A galaxy of business opportunities awaits! But where to begin your journey to wealth, fame, and glory? Relax. You can't rush success. Identify what sets you apart—what you have to offer that no one else has—and put together a plan to make it a reality that feels true to you. Take the example of a certain fashion forward smuggler-turned-planetary administrator-turned-rebel hero. He made it to the top thanks to a combination of networking, dressing to impress, and knowing how to play the game.

Be More Lando provides scoundrel-approved entrepreneurial tips from one of the suavest businessmen in the galaxy. In no time, you, too, will know how to keep cool and do it all.

GETTING STARTED

You want to make it big—or risk losing a floating city in the clouds trying. You're as hungry for success as a Sarlacc is for passersby. That ambition will serve you well, but the key to entrepreneurial triumph is discovering what you can offer that no one else has, and then developing a business plan to make it happen.

"Buckle up, baby."
Lando Calrissian

Go all in

You're just beginning, and the possibilities are endless. Total commitment is required. Half-measures mean your business's growth never makes the jump to hyperspeed, and you'll never achieve hyperwealth. Put everything on the line—even if that line is the edge of a black hole. Don't hedge your bets: whether at the sabacc table or in the boardroom when you're trying to get someone to sign on the dotted line. Lots of hard work is ahead, and the hardest part will be trying to make it look easy.

"There's always a bigger fish."
Qui-Gon Jinn

Understand the market

A business landscape is much like a food chain. You're motoring along, making progress, and suddenly a competitor tries to gobble you up like an opee sea killer with a suction-cup tongue. This industry rival is likely facing its own predator, too—a corporate sando aqua monster, perhaps. Research the market before you dive in, and with any luck, you can get your competitors to fight each other, leaving you room to grow.

"It's risky, but worth a try."
Qi'ra

Take risks

Playing it safe is a bit like folding in sabacc: you sacrifice a bit of your position so you won't lose a greater amount—but you'll never gain anything. Sometimes, you must be willing to back up your ambition with resources. If you're looking to invest in a start-up company or steal some hyperfuel from the gangsters who are technically supposed to be your allies, you have to realize you may lose your money—or worse, get caught up in a droid rebellion. But no risk, no reward.

"Welcome. I'm Lando Calrissian.
I'm the administrator
of this facility."
Lando Calrissian

Market Yourself

For people to take your business goals seriously, they need to take you seriously. So look the part, talk the talk, and walk the walk. Go for administrator attire over the smuggler look. Then speak with authority. Don't be afraid to talk yourself up. If you believe in yourself, others will believe in you, too. Maybe you'll even get to the point where you're so smooth you can make others think all is well, even when hidden stormtroopers have taken control of your city.

"Here goes nothing."
Lando Calrissian

Be inventive

Your value to the marketplace is equal to your best
idea. What's a detail you've noticed that no one else
has? If you're the only reason your entire fleet hasn't
slammed into a battle station's invisible deflector
shield, that means you are quite essential. Now, if you
can think of a solution no one else can, you might
really be onto something. Getting closer to enemy
star destroyers seems crazy—but it just might work!
New ideas drive success, and thinking outside the
box can mean more credits in your coffers.

PERFECTING YOUR BUSINESS PERSONA

There are as many different upstarts looking to hit it big as there are stars in the galaxy. And from a distance, all stars look the same. So how do you shine brighter than the rest? By breaking the mold and shining differently.

"You don't know a thing about me. Where I'm from. What I've seen."

Finn

Stand out from the crowd

Good branding usually means being yourself.
Figure out what makes you unique—your experience,
your skills, your flair for fashion—and develop those
things further. Even time you spent working sanitation
can save the galaxy if you learned how to lower a
superweapon's shields while mopping its floors.
There's comfort in conformity (everyone looks the
same behind stormtrooper armor) but standing out is
how you'll get noticed.

"There's no liars in this game, just players."
Lando Calrissian

Embrace euphemisms

Remember, the truths we cling to depend greatly
on our own point of view: some might call cheating
at cards deception—but you can call it creativity.
A little rule-bending shows you can think for yourself.
You may have allowed your friend to be frozen in
carbonite, but play up how he's now in a state of
perfect hibernation. A careful choice of words can
turn flaws into strengths, and that, my friend, is
how you can fit your talents to any proposal.

"I don't like it, I don't agree
with it, but I accept it."
Lando Calrissian

Be approachable

No one likes a reneging Rodian. It's important to
show that you're a reasonable businessperson; that
you're open to concessions. If a contractor you've
hired for a job suddenly springs a surprise out-of-
pocket expense on you, consider what you'll gain by
pulling out of the deal altogether. Probably nothing;
so don't cut off your proboscis to spite your face.
A concession now can mean a bigger gain
further down the hyperspace lane.

"Lando Calrissian. He's a card player, gambler, scoundrel. You'd like him."

Han Solo

Understand how others perceive you

Self-awareness is essential for growth. Part of that means being open—without ego—to learning how others view you. It will give you a sense of what parts of your persona need cultivation before positioning yourself in the galactic market. Just remember that these people could be wrong: they may think you're just a charming rogue with sharp sabacc skills and a flexible approach to cheating—they may not realize there's also a part of you that's a heroic rebel general just waiting to be unleashed.

"Yeah, I'm responsible these days. It's the price you pay for being successful."
Lando Calrissian

Talk the talk

Fake it 'til you make it. Stand tall and play it cool to
make others have confidence in you: they'll believe
you're in charge of a completely independent mining
facility that's escaped the notice of the Empire when,
in fact, that's not quite the case. Be unflappable,
professional, charming, and above all confident.
But don't veer into bravado—in case someone
has a particularly sharp poodoo detector.

NETWORKING

Expect to shake a lot of hands and tentacles. Introducing yourself to potential partners, clients, and customers expands your position in the market. Your business depends on the names stored in your holocomm. Add to this list constantly, but don't neglect your existing relationships, or they may disintegrate faster than Alderaan.

"Lucky for you there's exactly one guy I trust who can crack that kind of security. He's a master codebreaker, an ace pilot, a poet with a blaster …"

Maz Kanata

Let your reputation precede you

Not everyone has spare credits to spend on advertising: you probably won't be slapping your logo on a fathier jockey's silks at Canto Bight right away. But don't despair! Word of mouth is a highly effective form of promotion, and better yet, it's free! But to get people talking about you, you need to be memorable. So make a splash where you can, whether you're known for making risky but brilliant business decisions, being a security expert, or wearing a surprising variety of capes.

"Everything you've heard
about me is true."
Lando Calrissian

Never sell yourself short

It can be tempting to endear yourself with a self-deprecating joke, but making light of your accomplishments never works in business. If you're the best in the field, point it out. If you have industry-specific experience, don't be shy. If you pulled off a maneuver at the Battle of Taanab, make sure everybody knows it. Even a little self-mythologizing never hurt—*every* smuggler embellishes their résumé.

"I admire anyone who can crawl
their way out of a sewer."
Dryden Vos

Figure out what others can do for you

Nobody is a nobody. Whether they're a high-school dropout, a street kid hustling for a gangster worm on Corellia, or a person who has survived a few hours in the company of Jar Jar Binks, everyone has a story to tell. So don't judge a smuggler by his scruffiness— make the most of chance encounters to learn something new. Then you can benefit from the unique skills, experience, and insights your new friend has picked up along the way.

"Hello ... What have we here?"
Lando Calrissian

Make a strong first impression

An initial meeting can make or break you. Before interacting with anyone, take a look at yourself in the mirror and freshen up—make sure you don't have disheveled Wookiee hair or, worse, Wookiee breath. Dress to impress: a cape never hurts. Then, upon greeting your new acquaintance, make eye contact and mind your posture. Think about your choice of words: perhaps inject some personality into your business banter. Give your new contact something to remember about you.

"You look absolutely beautiful.
You truly belong here with
us among the clouds."

Lando Calrissian

Go on a charm offensive

Everyone loves a compliment. Adding that personal touch to your interactions can make all the difference. So don't be afraid to flash a smile and say something nice about your new acquaintance's recent project or their unusual Alderaanian hairstyle—you could even compliment their protocol droid. Just be mindful of coming on a little too strong: not everyone wants their hand kissed by someone they've just met.

WINNING THE BEST DEAL

The recipe for a perfect negotiation calls for research, timing, toughness, and leverage, though the exact ratios vary for each situation. Getting it just right is the difference between walking away with the *Millennium Falcon* ... or with just a meiloorun melon.

"Let me give you some
advice. Assume everyone
will betray you. And you will
never be disappointed."
Tobias Beckett

Know who you're dealing with

When ironing out the finer details of your business arrangement, the more you know about your partner the better. Don't rely on appearances: that's a guaranteed way to lose your ship and end up with a Sith Lord taking possession of your mining colony. It's better to be cautious. That's not to say you can't trust anyone: some people can be trusted to be untrustworthy. It's all about knowing the difference.

"You obviously have a
great deal to learn about
human behavior."
C-3PO

Understand how people think

Research is the single most important thing you
can do. What does your potential business partner
want? How will what you have help them attain that?
Whether it's the desire to reach a wider market,
the need to update their tech, or a fierce longing for
shiny gold plating and to never encounter sand again,
everyone wants something. If you can find out what
it is, you'll have the upper hand.

"No money, no parts!
No deal!"
Watto

Be a tough negotiator

No one respects a softie. You must negotiate with
confidence and conviction, and make sure everyone
knows that Jedi mind tricks won't work on you.
Whether you're negotiating for a higher fee, a faster
turnaround, a working hyperdrive, or the chance to
keep your friend from being frozen in carbonite, think
fast, stand strong, and talk big. Don't gamble it all
on the roll of your chance dice.

"Why you slimy, double-crossing,
no good swindler!"
Lando Calrissian

Say it like it is

Nobody should take advantage of you. Sadly, there
are people out there who would rather shoot under
the table than be a straight shooter. Make a name
for yourself as someone who is brutally honest.
Every business partner will know where they stand
with you, whether they're a new customer, a potential
supplier, or an old rival who rubs your face in past
grievances by asking for help in the very same
starship he won from you. Being forthright is good
for business. Plus, there's a certain amount of
satisfaction in calling a scoundrel a scoundrel.

"This deal is getting
worse all the time."
Lando Calrissian

Know when to back away

There's no shame in pulling out of a deal. Especially if the other party shows that they're unilaterally altering the original terms, and may alter them further. Better to take a step back, look at the situation objectively, and walk away—especially if they suddenly demand something outrageous, like the arrest and imprisonment of your guests. Not even a gleaming city in the clouds is worth keeping if you lose your self-respect.

ENJOYING YOUR SUCCESS

What's the point of working hard if you don't play hard, too? You didn't install that wet bar and cape closet on your ship for nothing. It's important to revel in all you've achieved so you feel satisfied and energized enough to seek out the next big score.

"That's a lot of capes."
Han Solo

Look good to feel good

You're confident, successful, and have accomplished all you have with style and flair. So why not dress with a little style and flair, too? Maybe a bantha wool coat for cold climates, and breathable Felucian fiber mesh for heat. But remember: what you wear isn't as important as how you wear it. Enough confidence and people will think your midi-chlorian count is higher than it really is. You don't need the closet of a Naboo queen to pull this off, though you really should have a cape for every occasion.

"Tell me you have a
backup plan."
Jyn Erso

Always have a plan B

You don't need to go so far as to build a spare
Death Star just in case your first one is destroyed,
but a backup plan is always advisable. It could mean
having an alternate method by which to achieve the
same goal, an ally in reserve who you wouldn't have
called upon otherwise, an emergency stash of cash if
you're suddenly short on credits, or, at the very least,
a workable double- or triple-cross that's only mildly
to moderately dangerous. Don't let yourself be undone
simply because you didn't think far enough ahead.

"Somehow I never get bored
with winning."
Tobias Beckett

Appreciate the good times

Take pleasure in your success. If you keep saying you want to spend a holiday on sunny Glee Anselm, take a holiday on sunny Glee Anselm. Suffering from work-related burnout is as detrimental as actually being burned by blaster fire. Plus, nothing says "boss" like frequent vacations. Make time for friends, take in a show, spend a little time telling tall tales in your memoirs. Just don't have too much fun and lose it all to an enraged Wookiee at dejarik.

"I'll get my people to
work on it."
Lando Calrissian

Learn the art of delegation

Part of being successful is having others know you're
in charge. Leaders lead. They don't have time to do
the small jobs—nor do they want to. Get yourself a
Lobot. Give enough direction to show everyone who's
boss, and then relax and focus on the bigger picture
while your underlings do the grunt work for you.
If you can somehow give complex commands
via a comlink on your wrist, all the better.

"Might want to quit while
you're ahead."
Lando Calrissian

Stop at the top

When you achieve all you've ever wanted—wealth,
fame, a personal style envied by all others—it can
be tempting to keep reaching for more.
WAIT. STOP. NO.
Don't smuggle any more spice or steal more coaxium.
Taking risks may have helped get you where you
are, but taking more may cause you to lose it all.
Enjoy being at the top, and seek that risk-taking thrill
elsewhere. Like in a game of cards or local politics.

Project Editor Shari Last
Project Art Editor Jon Hall
Pre-production Producer Siu Yin Chan
Senior Producer Mary Slater
Managing Editor Sadie Smith
Managing Art Editor Vicky Short
Publisher Julie Ferris
Art Director Lisa Lanzarini
Publishing Director Simon Beecroft

DK would like to thank: Sammy Holland, Michael Siglain, Jennifer Heddle,
Troy Alders, Leland Chee, Matt Martin, Pablo Hidalgo, Nicole LaCoursiere,
Bryce Pinkos, Erik Sanchez, and Kelly Jensen at Lucasfilm; Chelsea Alon
at Disney Publishing; and Megan Douglass for proofreading.

First American Edition, 2019
Published in the United States by DK Publishing
1450 Broadway, Suite 801, New York, NY 10018

DK books are available at special discounts when purchased in bulk for sales promotions,
premiums, fund-raising, or educational use. For details, contact: DK Publishing Special
Markets, 1450 Broadway, Suite 801, New York, NY 10018. SpecialSales@dk.com

Printed and bound in China

A WORLD OF IDEAS:
SEE ALL THERE IS TO KNOW

www.dk.com
www.starwars.com